THE EASY PIANO COLLECTION
DEBUSSY
GOLD

Published by:
Chester Music Limited,
14-15 Berners Street, London W1T 3LJ, UK.

Exclusive Distributors:
Music Sales Limited,
Distribution Centre, Newmarket Road, Bury St Edmunds, Suffolk IP33 3YB, UK.
Music Sales Corporation,
257 Park Avenue South, New York, NY10010, United States of America.
Music Sales Pty Limited,
120 Rothschild Avenue, Rosebery, NSW 2018, Australia.

Order No. CH74591
ISBN 978-1-84772-818-0
This book © Copyright 2009 by Chester Music.

Edited by Jenni Wheeler.
New arrangements by Jeremy Birchall, Christopher Hussey & Simon Townley.

Printed in the EU.

Your Guarantee of Quality:
As publishers, we strive to produce every book to the highest commercial standards.
The music has been freshly engraved and carefully designed to minimise
awkward page turns to make playing from it a real pleasure.
Particular care has been given to specifying acid-free, neutral-sized
paper made from pulps which have not been elemental chlorine bleached.
This pulp is from farmed sustainable forests and was produced
with special regard for the environment.
Throughout, the printing and binding have been planned to ensure a sturdy,
attractive publication which should give years of enjoyment.
If your copy fails to meet our high standards, please inform us and we will gladly replace it.

www.musicsales.com

CHESTER MUSIC
part of the Music Sales Group

London/New York/Paris/Sydney/Copenhagen/Berlin/Madrid/Tokyo

Après Fortune Faite/Epilogue
(from Tableau 4, from 'La boîte à joujoux')
Page 6

Arabesque No.1
(from 'Two Arabesques')
Page 10

Clair De Lune
(from 'Suite Bergamasque')
Page 12

Danse Bohémienne
Page 18

Des Pas Sur La Neige
(Steps On The Snow) (from 'Préludes Book 1')
Page 15

En Bateau
(Boating) (from 'Petite Suite')
Page 22

Golliwogg's Cakewalk
(from 'Children's Corner')
Page 26

Hommage À Rameau
(Homage To Rameau) (from 'Images Pour Piano, Book 1')
Page 34

La Fille Aux Cheveux De Lin
(The Girl With The Flaxen Hair) (from 'Préludes Book 1')
Page 31

The Little Shepherd (from 'Children's Corner')
Page 38

Mazurka
Page 41

Minuet (from 'Suite Bergamasque')
Page 44

Passepied (from 'Suite Bergamasque')
Page 46

Pour Invoquer Pan, Dieu Du Vent D'été
(from 'Six Épigraphes Antiques')
Page 49

Prélude À L'après-midi D'un Faune (Opening)
Page 52

Rêverie
Page 56

String Quartet in G minor, Op.10
(3rd Movement)
Page 62

Valse Romantique
Page 59

Claude Debussy

It was the exhibition in 1963 of Monet's painting 'Sunrise; An Impression' that ultimately gave birth to the term 'impressionism'. Though it was a term Debussy did not like, it was suitable in that composers were obscuring the traditions of 'exhausted' harmony with new sonorities and colours, just as painters were obscuring the outlines of objects with gentle fogs and mists, or with the fuzzy reflection of street lights through an evening's drizzle of rain. The symbolist poet Mellarmé said, 'To name an object is to...sacrifice enjoyment...To *suggest* it—that is our dream.' Perhaps this explains why, in the original score, the *Piano Preludes'* titles appear at the *end* of each piece, allowing an aural image to suggest itself before the identification of a scene, smell of a scent, or the invocation of a wonderful sound. *Gardens In Rain, Reflections In The Water, Dead Leaves, Dialogue Of The Wind And The Sea* are typical of the array of poetic titles to be found in his output.

Achille-Claude Debussy was born in 1862, Saint-Germain-en-Laye and was the eldest of three brothers and a sister. His parents ran a little china shop before moving to Clichy and then to Rue Pigalle in Paris. Times were hard, and whilst his siblings were taken in by his aunt, he was left to his own education and could not attend school. His brother Eugene died of meningitis when seven years old, and Claude and his sister were taken to Cannes. At the tender age of eight, he is described as being introspective, a boy who spent whole days sitting on a chair thinking. He collected colourful butterflies (arranging them in zigzags on his bedroom wall) and thought of becoming a painter.

In Cannes, he received piano lessons, and Mme Mauté de Fleurville (a former pupil of Chopin) pronounced that he should become a musician. Thus he entered the Paris Conservatoire aged ten, socially awkward and initially disliked. He adored the music of Berlioz, Wagner, Mussorgsky and Lalo (once being escorted out of a theatre for being too enthusiastic) and abhorred Beethoven. In the summers of 1881 and 1882 he worked for Tchaikovsky's patron, Mme von Meck, in Russia. He failed to win the renowned Prix de Rome in 1883 but succeeded the following year and was to spend three years composing in the Villa Medici, meeting other artists such as Liszt, Verdi and Boito, but he found this a miserable experience and returned a year early. In 1894, he composed the tone-poem *Prélude à L'Après-midi d'un Faune* (The Afternoon of a Fawn) based on Mellarmé's poem, which, along with his only *String Quartet*, ensured much public discussion. At the age of 40, his opera *Pelléas et Mélisande* offered confirmation that there was a composer changing musical history—the lyricism of his vocal writing and lack of movements made many feel the experience to be like one massive recitative. The writer, Maeterlinck, furiously and publicly wished it to be an 'emphatic failure'.

By many, Debussy was classed 'second rate' and unusual', but it took little time for his individuality to be indelibly established as the voice of a genius. He did not really care about the expected rules and formulae of the past as revealed when submitting a composition as a student. His tutor, Émile Rély, demanded, 'Dissonant chords do not have to be resolved? What rules do you follow?' to which Debussy famously replied, 'Mon plaisir!' His use of large orchestral forces was not for sakes of power but for delicate employment of tone-colour, and subtle effects of motion and stillness. His overall 'impressionistic' sound perhaps comes from his use of the whole-tone scale—sonorities that were unusually atmospheric and far removed from the mainstream harmony and the rich chromaticism of Wagner and Strauss. He turned away from the Classical era's rigid forms, and was drawn to a more refined offering of emotion than was present in the Romantic era before him.

The piano music of Debussy was inspired by the younger Ravel's *Jeux d'eau* (1901) that offered a new realm of possibility into the world of technical skill and imaginative sound. (Compare *Pour le Piano* with the illuminated *Images*). Outside of the 'big piano works' that took the instrument through a renaissance, are the delightful smaller pieces, many of which are in this album. *Rêverie* was written in a hurry in 1890, yet its melodic innocence remains a delight today. *Petite Suite*, written in 1889 was for two pianos in the style of Fauré, and *Children's Corner* was written for Claude-Emma, his illegitimate daughter. *Golliwogg's Cakewalk*, from this work, was an African-American dance that made fun of white society's mannerisms.

He said that he would write his memoirs in his 60s, but he developed cancer in 1910, was a near invalid by 1914, and died when he was 55, in 1918.

Quentin Thomas

Dictionary of some of the French terms used in this book

Assez animé	Quite animated
Au mouvement	With movement
Ce rythme doit avoir la valeur sonore d'un fond paysage triste et glacé	This rhythm must have the sonority of a sad and frozen landscape
Cédez	Slower
Cédez avec un grand émotion	Slower with a great feeling
Comme un tendre et triste regret	Like a tender and sad regret
Doucement expressif	Gently expressive
Doux et expressif	Soft and expressive
En animant surtout dans l'expression	Especially animated in expression
Expressif	Expressively
Expressif et doucement soutenu	Expressive and gently sustained
Expressif et douloureux	Expressive and painful
Expressif et tendre	Expressive and tender
Légèrement et expressif	Lightly and expressive
Lent et grave (dans le style d'une Sarabande mais sans rigueur)	Slow and solemn (in the style of a Sarabande but without the strictness)
Marqué	Marked
m.d. (main droite)	Right hand
Même mouvement, joyeux et éclatant	Same movement, merry and bright
m.g. (main gauche)	Left hand
Plus lent	Slower
Plus mouvement	More movement
Retenez/Retenu	Hold back (ritenuto)
Toujours retenu	Always held back (sempre ritenuto)
Très delicament	Very delicately
Très doux et délicatement expressif	Very softly and delicately expressive
Très modéré	Very moderately
Très net et très sec	Very clear and very dry
Très soutenu	Very sustained
Triste et lent	Sad and slow
*Un peu marqué mais toujours **pp***	A little marked but always **pp**
Un peu moins vite	A little less quickly
Un peu plus lent	A little less slow
Un peu retenu (en conservant le rythme)	A little held back (keeping the rhythm)

Après Fortune Faite/Epilogue
(from Tableau 4, from 'La boîte à joujoux')

Composed by Claude Debussy

APRÈS FORTUNE FAITE
Tempo di Polka

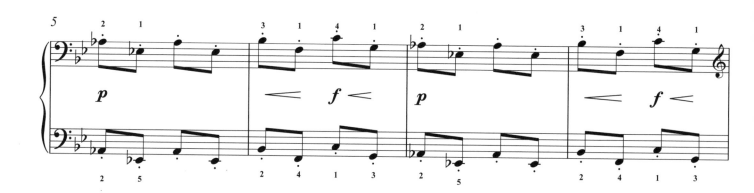

Même mouvement, joyeux et éclatant

EPILOGUE

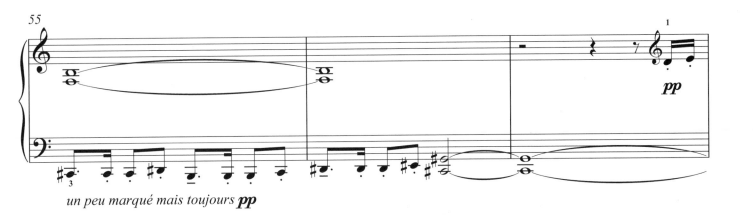

un peu marqué mais toujours **pp**

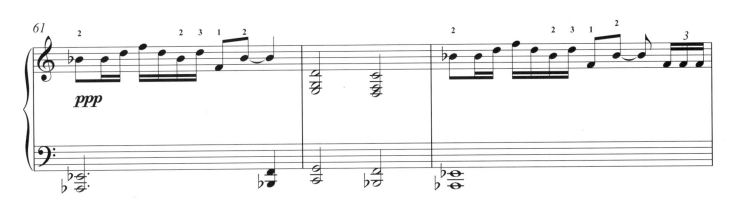

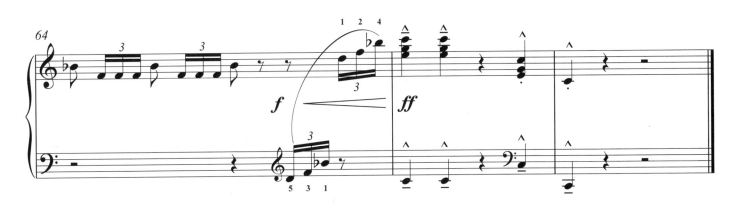

Arabesque No.1
(from 'Two Arabesques')

Composed by Claude Debussy

a tempo

Clair De Lune
(from 'Suite Bergamasque')

Composed by Claude Debussy

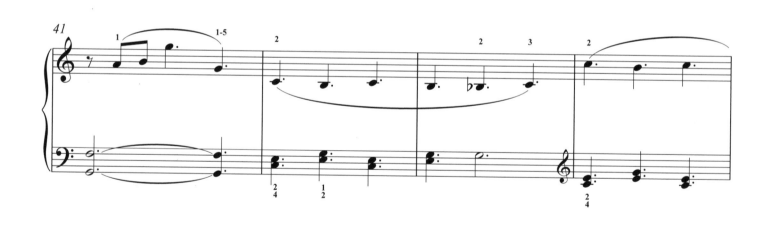

Des Pas Sur La Neige (Steps On The Snow)
(from 'Préludes Book 1')

Composed by Claude Debussy

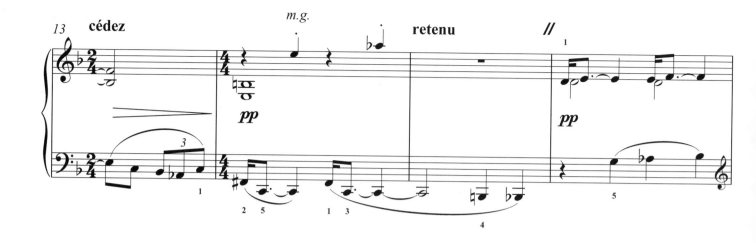

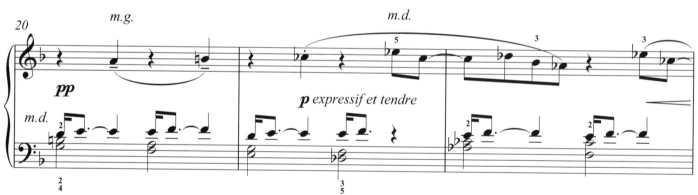

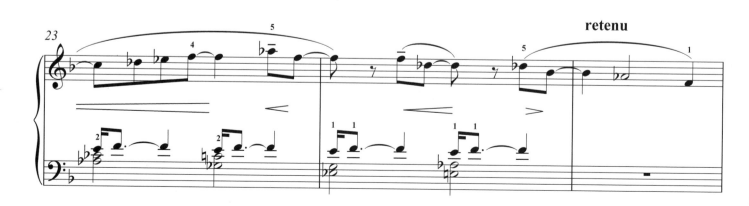

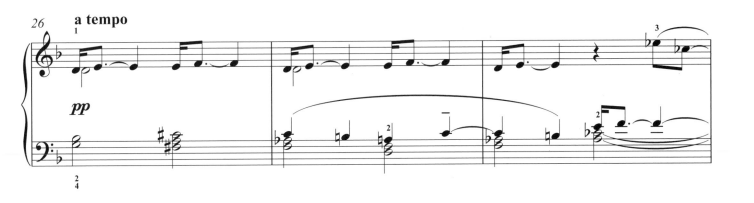

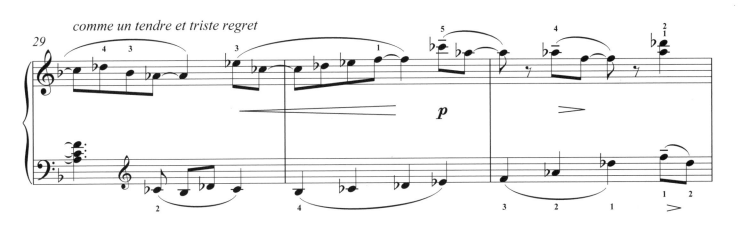

Danse Bohémienne

Composed by Claude Debussy

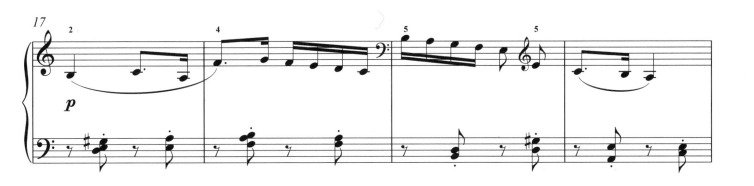

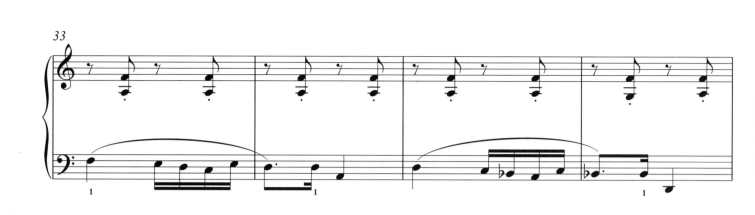

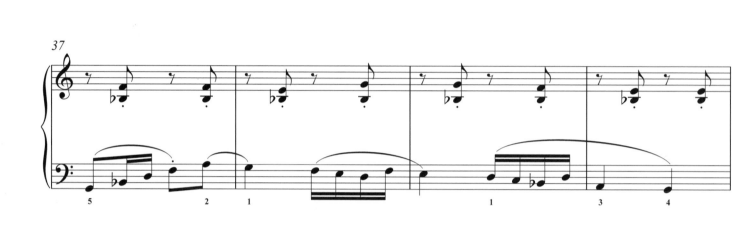

D.C. al Coda

✛ **Coda**

En Bateau (Boating)
(from 'Petite Suite')

Composed by Claude Debussy

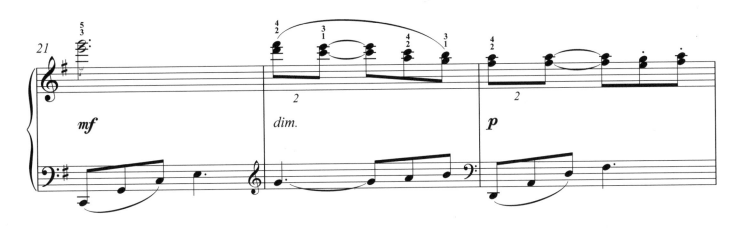

To Coda ⊕

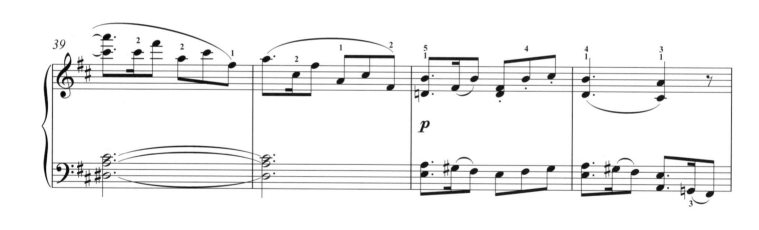

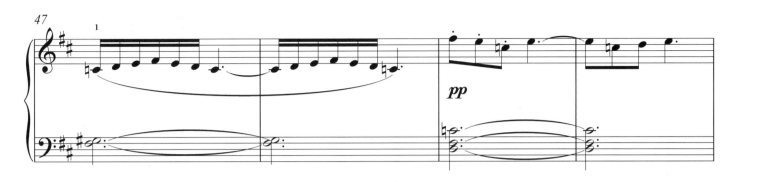

D.C. al Coda

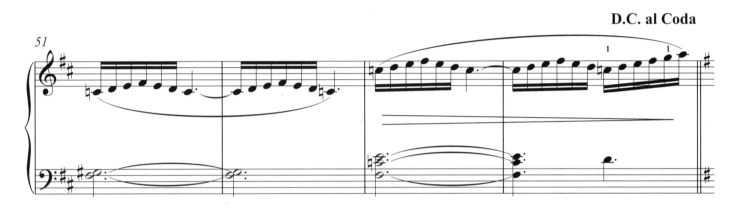

✛ Coda

Golliwogg's Cakewalk
(from 'Children's Corner')

Composed by Claude Debussy

Allegro giusto

Très net et très sec

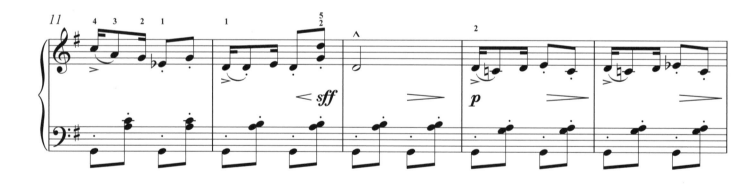

to Coda ⊕

29

La Fille Aux Cheveux De Lin
(The Girl With The Flaxen Hair)
(from 'Préludes Book 1')

Composed by Claude Debussy

Very calm and sweetly expressive

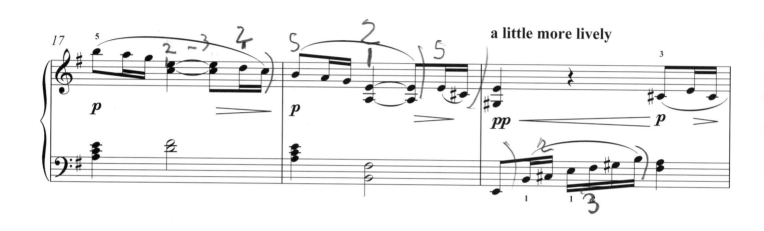

a little more lively

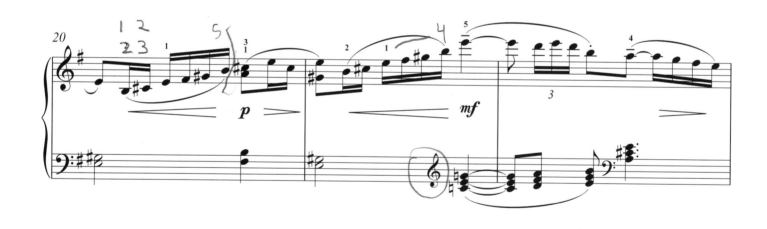

Tempo I

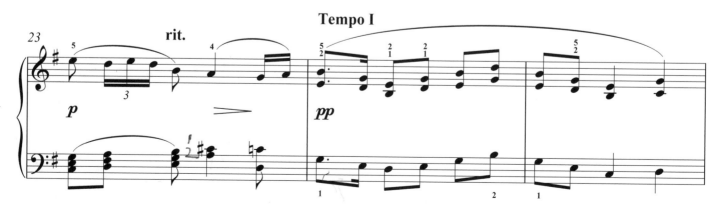

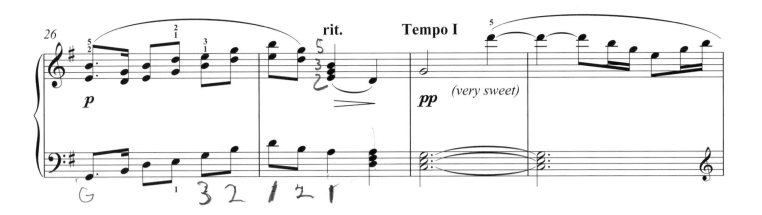

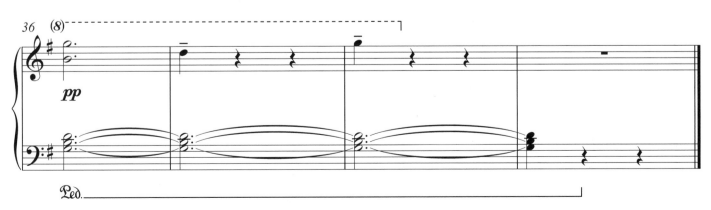

Hommage À Rameau (Homage To Rameau)
(from 'Images Pour Piano, Book 1')

Composed by Claude Debussy

Lent et grave
(dans le style d'une Sarabande mais sans rigueur)

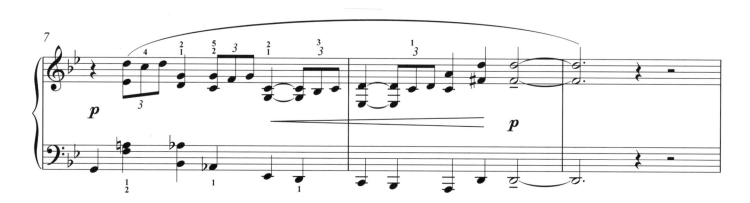

The Little Shepherd
(from 'Children's Corner')

Composed by Claude Debussy

Très modéré

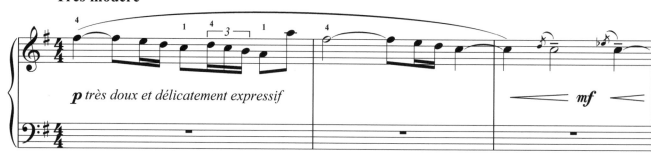

Plus mouvement

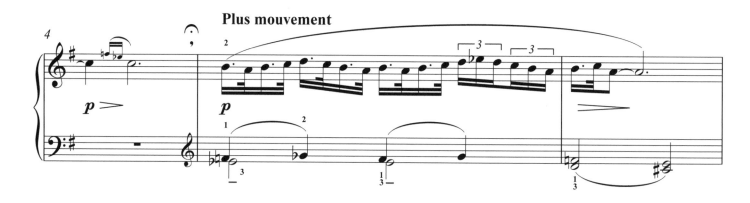

au mouvement

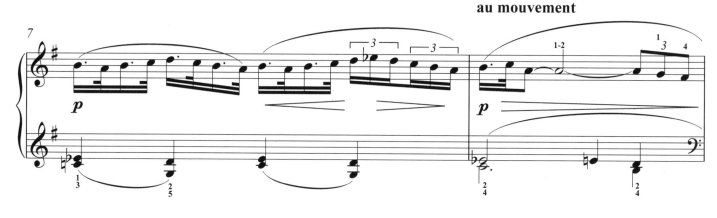

Cédez _ _ _ _ _ _ _ _ _ **//**

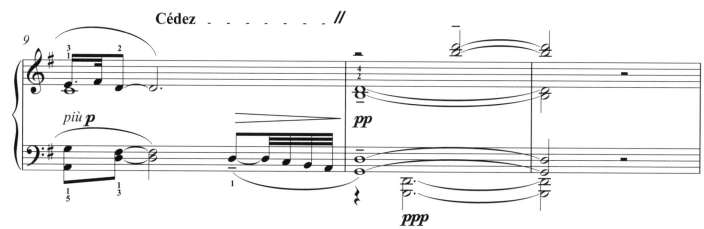

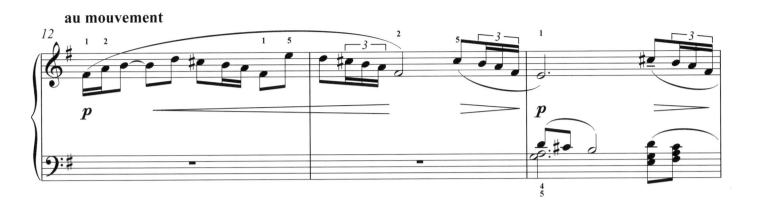

au mouvement

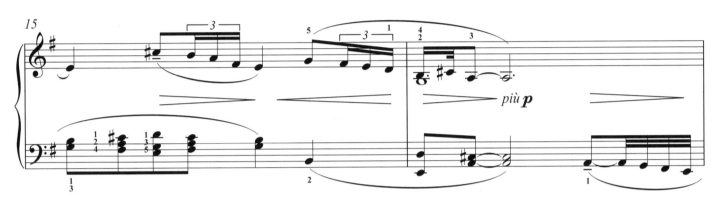

Cédez - - - - - - - -

- - - - - - - - - - - - - - **au mouvement**

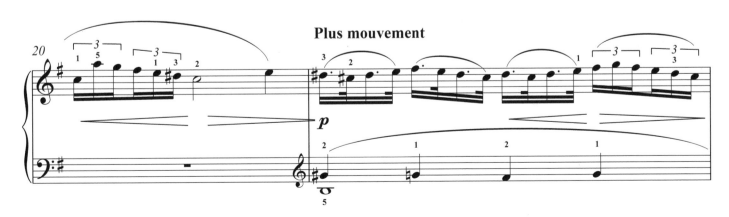

Plus mouvement

Poco animato

crescendo poco a poco

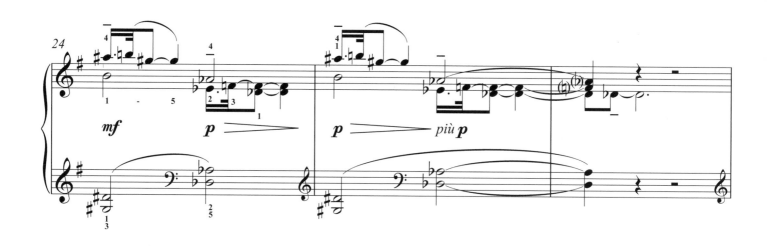

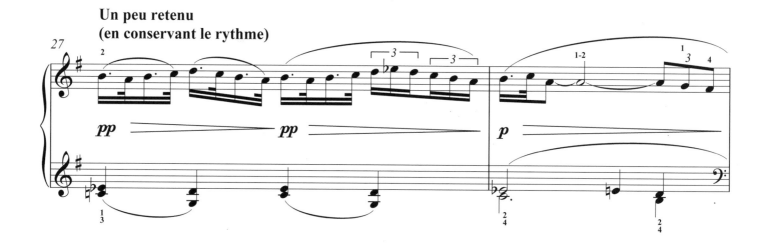

Un peu retenu
(en conservant le rythme)

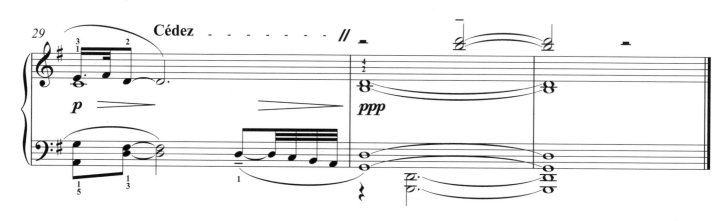

Cédez - - - - - - - - **//**

Mazurka

Composed by Claude Debussy

Scherzando (assez animé)

Meno tempo

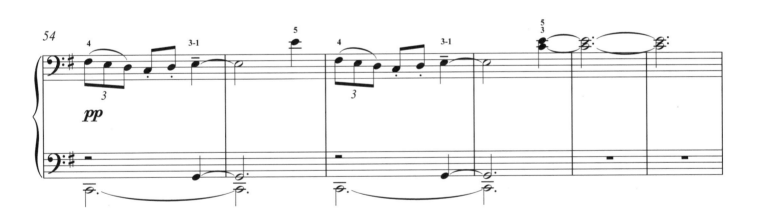

a tempo stringendo   **Vivo**

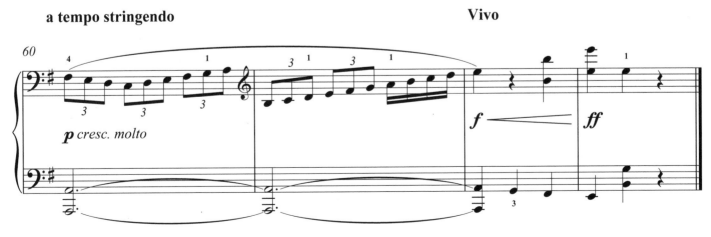

Minuet
(from 'Suite Bergamasque')

Composed by Claude Debussy

Andantino

Passepied
(from 'Suite Bergamasque')

Composed by Claude Debussy

Allegretto ma non troppo

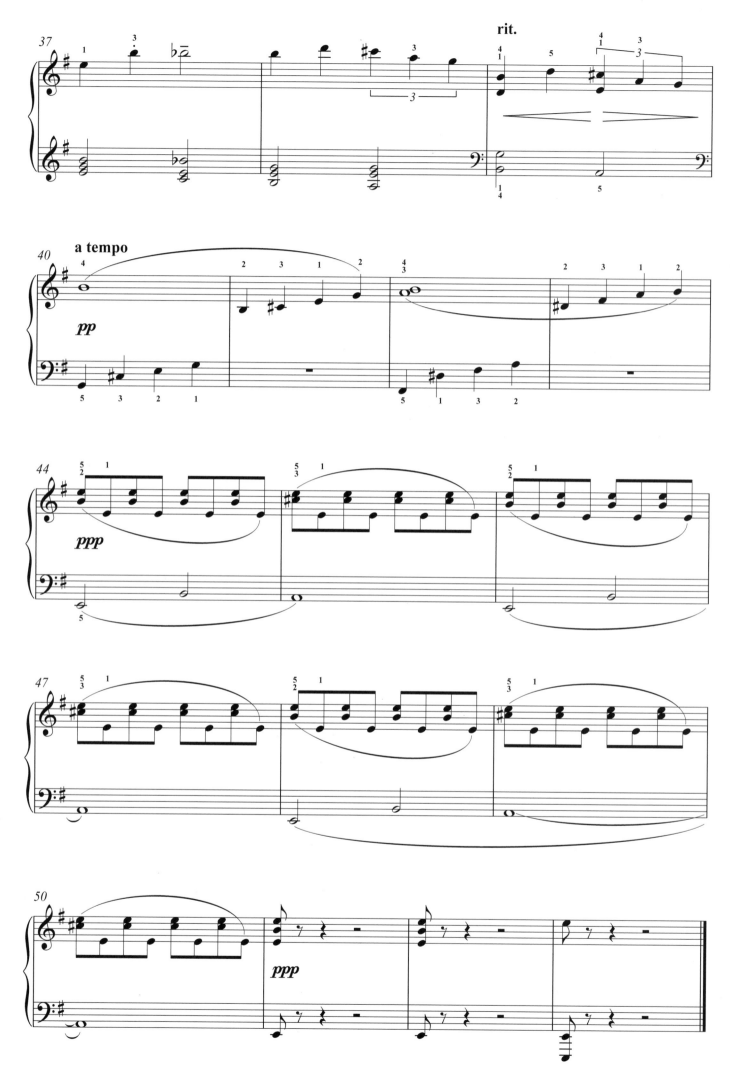

Pour Invoquer Pan, Dieu Du Vent D'été
(from 'Six Épigraphes Antiques')

Composed by Claude Debussy

Moderato, in a pastoral style

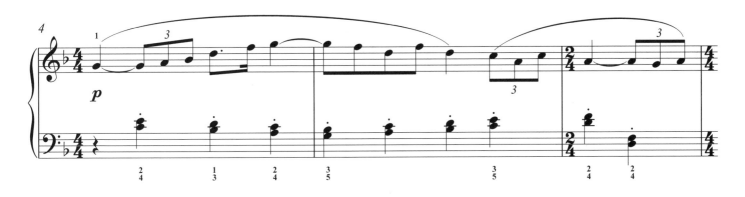

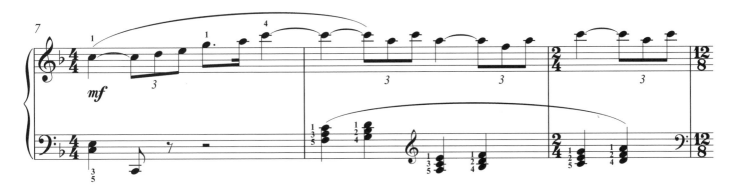

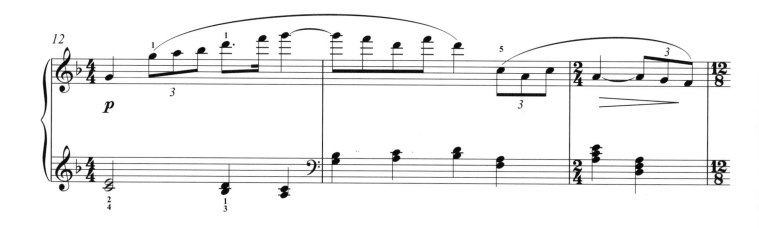

Slowing down

A little faster

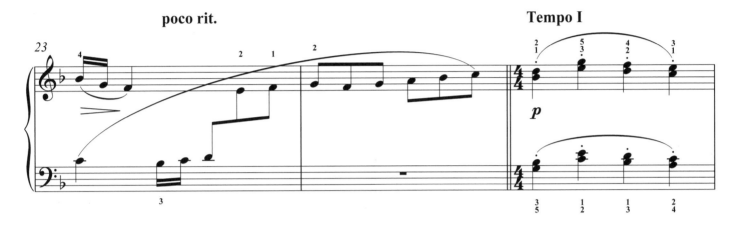

poco rit.

Tempo I

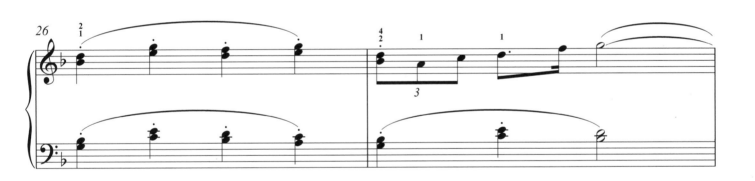

Slower

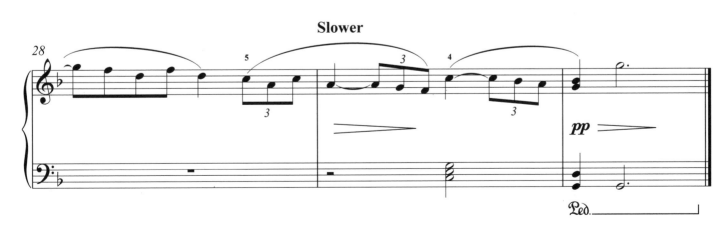

Prélude À L'après-midi D'un Faune
(Opening)

Composed by Claude Debussy

Très modéré

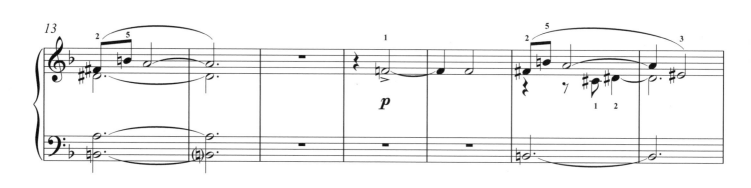

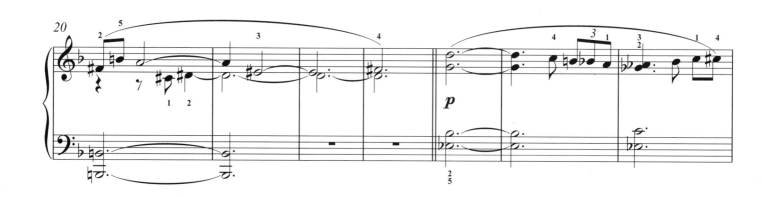

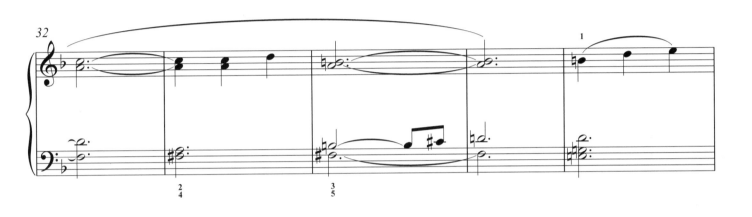

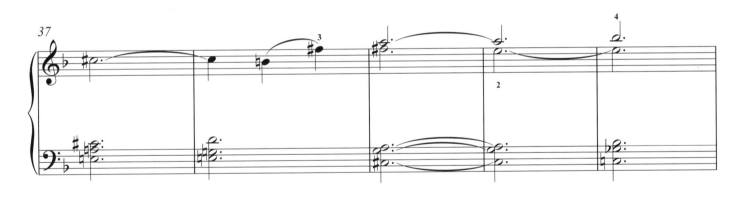

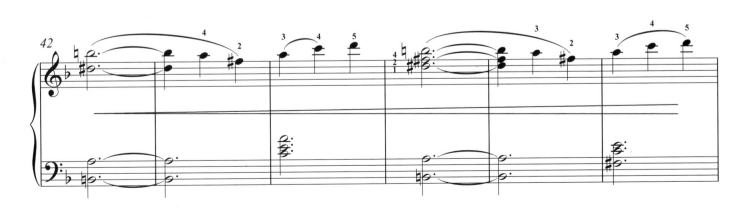

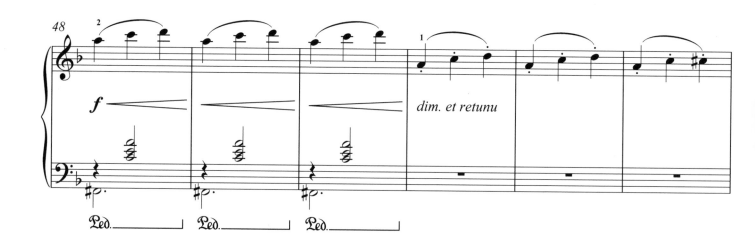

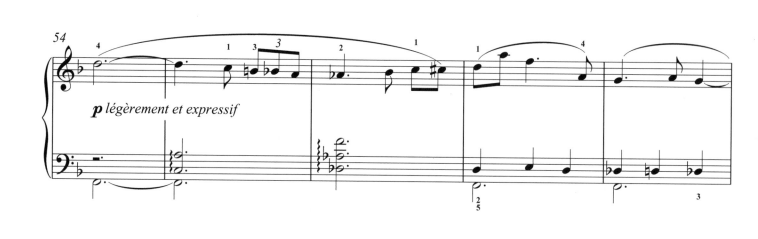

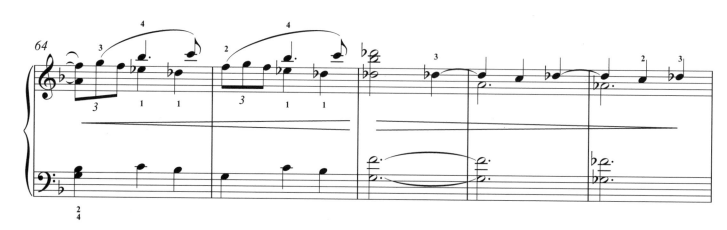

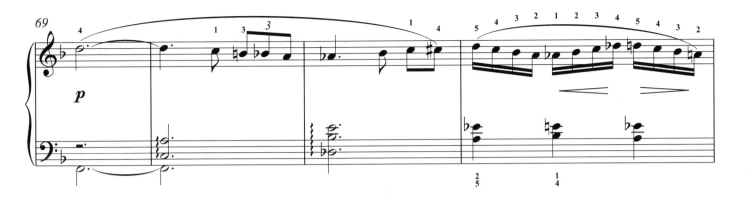

Rêverie

Composed by Claude Debussy

D.S. al Coda $\oplus$ **Coda**

Valse Romantique

Composed by Claude Debussy

Tempo di valse (Allegro moderato)

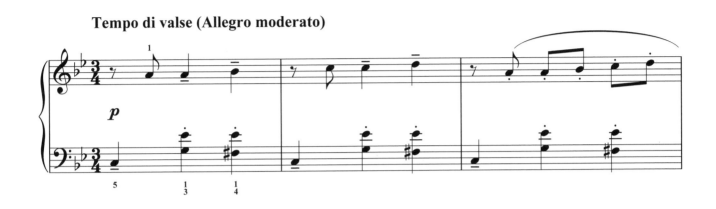

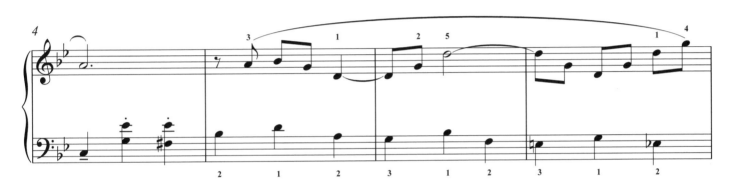

Moto

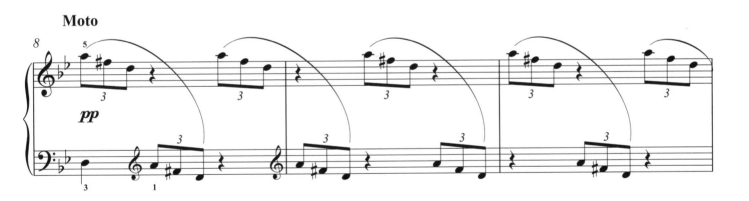

poco rit.   **a tempo**

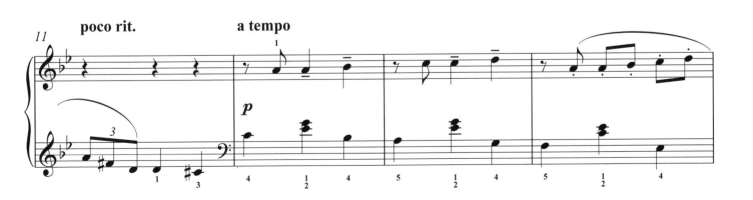

Tempo 1

String Quartet in G minor, Op.10
(3rd Movement)

Composed by Claude Debussy

Andantino, doucement expressif

123456789

Bringing you the words and the music

All the latest music in print... rock & pop plus jazz, blues, country, classical and the best in West End show scores.

- Books to match your favourite CDs.

- Book-and-CD titles with high quality backing tracks for you to play along to. Now you can play guitar or piano with your favourite artist... or simply sing along!

- Audition songbooks with CD backing tracks for both male and female singers for all those with stars in their eyes.

- Can't read music? No problem, you can still play all the hits with our wide range of chord songbooks.

- Check out our range of instrumental tutorial titles, taking you from novice to expert in no time at all!

- Musical show scores include *The Phantom Of The Opera*, *Les Misérables*, *Mamma Mia* and many more hit productions.

- DVD master classes featuring the techniques of top artists.